Presocratic Blues

Joel Bettridge

chax
2009

Published by Chax Press
411 N 7th Ave Ste 103
Tucson Arizona 85705

ISBN 9780925904827

for Nathan and for Kim

Contents

I. Testimonia

Heraclitus wakes having dreamt of the flux
"At the grocery Melissus stares at the checkout girl"
"Not able to find his favorite swimming hole Heraclitus"
After treating a patient for yet another unknown ailment...
Thales takes a turn at the pulpit
Diogenes and Stagolee in a Punch-Up
"Across the room Zeno takes"
Archelaus, at his front stoop, considers
"At the Sunday School teachers' curriculum meeting"
"Protagoras gets fired off the job"
"Philolaus walking through the park sees a youth"
"Anaximenes puts a knife in Thales"
His theory of *becoming* having failed...
"'The strangeness,' Anaximander taught"
"Democritus scratches at the bathroom stall"
Prodicus Buries His Cat
"That night Democritus puts on Billie Holiday"
At church Xenophanes hears...
Democritus speaks of ranch-style homes
"Critias, on the difference between gods and men"
Eurytus, having drunk too much...

II. Hollers

I

TESTIMONIA

Democritus and Heraclitus were two philosophers, of whom the first, finding the condition of man vain and ridiculous, never went out in public but with a mocking and laughing face; whereas Heraclitus, having pity and compassion on this same condition of ours, wore a face perpetually sad, and eyes filled with tears. . . . I prefer the first humor; not because it is pleasanter to laugh than to weep, but because it is more disdainful, and condemns us more than the other; and it seems to me that we can never be despised as much as we deserve.

— Montaigne, "Of Democritus and Heraclitus"

Heracleitus wakes having dreamt of the flux

no borrowed light for some reason
to circle about us
that breadth of a man's foot
in repose
the night
comes slipping in
these other stars don't suffice
to make me glad
what flows what abides not
what gives way
what stays
not fixed
even if—hey—
we are small ordered worlds and
we're gonna need somebody when

* * *

At the grocery Melissus stares at the checkout girl by reading the magazine behind her.

He goes home and writes:
"thought and being, being the same, I haven't had an agreeable time thinking of you."

At breakfast he writes:
"that you could not care to take me home or stay here much longer
makes me think wisdom is too much distilled from moral necessity."

When she smiles at him the next time he buys half & half he writes in the car on the
back of an envelope:
"the present unpleasantness of waiting out my own interest";

on the back of a student paper:
"wondering tonight how much I don't care, wondering what will be enough to make facility a
mistress of mine."

That night he imagines he talks to her and gets into her underthings by asking if
she knows the difference between "seems" and "is."

He wakes up later and scratches on a receipt on his desk:
"the day's verdict that pleases me best is not to think of you, when I turn, conceivably
toss, myself before I, want to say fall, I'd say uselessly—asleep."

After treating a patient for yet another unknown ailment Hippocrates records a Note-to-Self

these times all of us is tired, these times
all of us creep away

those substances
such as cold and sunlight and the inconstant restless winds

like reproductive fluid, which is a form of bile and
must be gotten out

for with it we drain sadness and burdens lay to rest

like the calcification of someone's face in everyone
else's

Thales takes a turn at the pulpit

Why not
be not able to hide from that
which never sets
from that which moves too much
tonight
that boy
we follow
we stumble behind
not knowing whither
we goes

*   *   *

Not able to find his favorite swimming hole Heraclitus
eats the lunch he's packed in the parking lot and reasons
"there must be a better way to proceed than this."
Later
Anaxagoras slurs into his ear: "Heracli, listen,
don't you see
everything is made of everything, but the object it is has most of that,"
and Heraclitus thinks
"avert from my tongue the madness of such men";
he thinks
"if I could get a few more dollars
I could get those forty acres
and grow my olives in peace."

Diogenes and Stagolee in a Punch-Up

Over a body with a bullet through its eye
Stag mutters:

"Your stars leave me unsatisfied
and the proposition 'all's of atmosphere'
isn't much to calculate;
there is proportions, and
the angle of deflection;
there's geographic boundaries and
property divisions;
there's need for practical ways of
figuring perpendiculars
without the outer joints of the thumb, or the length of a stride.
What of how far off ships at sea? What of
my hope for superimposements repeatedly,
without breaks or overlapping?"

Oh cruel Stagolee, you're a bad man
even if you're right.

Across the room Zeno takes
the longest trip in the history of the whole world by
going to get a water back there from the sink

Archelaus, at his front stoop, considers

The mind is like the air, or is
the air more like
the man who gets my pay who
doesn't even look that much like me, who
already can't make enough to make up for what
gives us
us in a colloquial and even in a formal shape, I'm
assured there was a certain mixture
I was given confident words as to the benefits of hard work
and
applying what is known
in the burgeoning field of physics
to those older ethics—

it is not so cordial a time it seems
to stand in for the decline of a point of view.

* * *

At the Sunday school teachers' curriculum meeting Antiphon and Mississippi John Hurt argue for different approaches to early childhood education:

Antiphon opens by saying, "it is important they learn to sin not against the gods nor confound the ordinances of man; it is important they know that it is not the common needs of the individual we should attend to, but concord and self-restraint within communities, and within the single soul."

Being more in the mood for practical application John Hurt responds, "my burdens I've laid down; my sickness, my sorrow, they've been laid down."

A politician, interpreter of dreams, would-be squarer of the circle, and possibly a tragedian, Antiphon says, "when God was minded to create the human race and brought the first of us into being, he gave us the earth and the sea to sustain and serve us, in order that we might not die for want of the necessaries of life before old age brought us our end. What we are talking about here are fundamentals—those truths a life can be circled around."

John Hurt says, "I've not had time to think on it, I've not had time from the sick soil, the crops that need to come around again. I'm as a wanderer, like the sun that goeth down; that darkness that be over me; my rest that be in stone."

He says, "I've only had time to turn my ear; a moment between; angels you see, they beckon me, nearer, those angels, beckon, nearer, you see."

*   *   *

Protagoras gets fired off the job for using his torso as a measuring tape
and is struck by a bus that afternoon clad only in a bicycle helmet and his underpants.
Responsible for deaths by city property
the municipal authorities stack phonebooks under his feet,
the coffin they laid him in having been built for a taller man who later recovered from his
    infirmity.

His theory of *becoming* having failed, Philolaus seeks an answer to his puzzlement from the Oracle at Delphi who channels Bessie Smith

At least it's a day distinguished like every other
in knowing in the end that everyone will be in a right damn fix,
a house we can't live in no more
a tongue that echoes, the intelligence only in what encompasses us
a dialectic that can't understand itself
and even still you find enough trouble to make a poor girl wonder where to go.

*   *   *

Democritus scrapes at the bathroom stall:
"by convention there is sweet,
by convention there is bitter,
by convention hot and cold, by convention color,
but in reality there are only atoms and the void."
He peels back the paint from the metal with his key
and calls Michelle for what is promised who
tells him not to believe everything he reads.

Anaximenes puts a knife in Thales for saying
everything is made of water rather than air—
"gone to Jesus" he says
"we're all gone to Jesus."

*   *   *

"The strangeness," Anaximander taught, "of someone you've seen without clothes on"; "remarkable" he said, "when she talks as if you hadn't."

He said "what appears to have no limit emerges and then perishes to make reparation for its injustice."

The first to attempt a scientific method, and the first to think in spheres, Anaximander is known to have asked a young Anaximenes, calling to sell him insurance, "but suppose what makes full use of me is not my recollection of the way I'd hoped to moderately push my mouth between what is measured by those contraptions I've first invented—the sun dial, a map of the known world, and the first charts of where the stars live."

Standing in lines he had no need of, he would ask the man behind him, "what becomes of winter when summer takes its place?"

He said, "I'm separated off, in general, even if there is no one to blame but me, except you, maybe, I tend toward natural science, geometry and astronomy. I figure it would not be better if minutes happened to men just as they wish."

*   *   *

Philolaus walking through the park sees a youth who reminds him of his dead boyfriend.
Arriving home he makes a journal entry headed, "My Dead Boyfriend."
It reads, "harmonia, described mathematically, must
still be of use here; the continuum of sound can't be entirely out of place, or ratios
either, or what sits in the center of what we stand on.

To be exact, it is necessary that whole formulas be bonded together by the octave, the fifth, or
the fourth, or the bellybutton, which I remember best.
What a disproportion he had on him. Does that put all my subsequent
theses in question? I wonder if he still would
like he used to do?"

Prodicus Buries His Cat

Who is left to say "it appears" and "it is perceived"?
Who will be the one to say these might not necessarily
amount to the same thing?

Who can notice now what is accepted as a bullet in the brain for one and
not for another who does not experience it so?

Who is left to convince a man that what once was less than good is
now much better?

Who will bother to explain to the gods that they do
or do not

exist
and are of little use in most forms they take?

And who will stand now to tell a joke
that discriminates

between synonyms and gives us something to do
when we sit

staring
at the back of our heads?

* * *

That night Democritus puts on Billie Holiday
and does philosophy instead—he scribbles:

What I know is ex-wife-like
and flows into us and don't explain
even more than once
the shift in character
that goes according to dispositions and
confrontations.

He crosses that out and tries again:

Hush my amusement
each occurrence is or is not
my discomfort
and let me just to haul myself to bed
don't matter these
roaming thoughts
that come back to me with lipstick on their collars.

At church Xenophanes hears of Danae having just been ravished by a cloud-burst

I can't tell who it is
just left my bed
quite evidently, salvation
is not revealed at the outset.

Democritus speaks of ranch-style homes

We've known ranch-style homes:
We've known ranch-style homes with nice use of natural light and backyards with plenty of
room to barbeque in.

We've grown accustomed like a ranch-style home.

I've discerned that a long, low roofline creates informal, casual living.
I've found that stucco is convenient to maintain and looks attractive in the landscape.
I've surmised that sliding glass entries and exits grant me a functional relationship to the
out-of-doors (just as I once accepted that atomic behavior can't be named).
I've learned that a simple, open floor plan allows me to rearrange rooms to serve multiple
purposes, like watching the early news while toasting bread hot and crisp so it can
melt the morning's butter right away.

We've known ranch-style homes:
relatively new, with generous square feet, ranch style-homes.

We've grown accustomed, like a ranch-style home.

(Critias, on the difference between gods and men)

It's relatively easy to score that is
when you can open cans without touching them
and when you don't think about your penis as a wing-man.

Eurytus, having drunk too much, is most himself when speaking

Those who postulate relationships
or explain objects as if we are recipes,

your legs, for instance, or moral outlook,
more like paprika or a pinch of cinnamon;

as if a square had anything to do with four,
rather than being four itself, or what

all the teeth in your jaw add up to be
called half of;

to be composed of numbers,
to need training other than being an empty into

to need finding employment to sustain
kinships, and don't become such and what again,

but good luck, you are a small colored stone
on a wall stood up with plaster

you are two hundred and fifty, and your
favorite spider plant is 360, like the circle.

At cards Hippocrates and Blind Willie Johnson discuss a point of epistemology

What of fevers? Are they too of gods? What of ailments of the liver?
Blame your welfare on one of them if you like but don't expect to get any better—
the breeze might be holy but the chill it gives you isn't.

At least allow that a man is of no single substance: to see the case it is enough to examine
the conflicts within him or the infirmities he's managed to garner. Pain
it comes from excessive presence or in evacuation.
A method of procedure is what we need to get our theories on straight.

Halt what illness flourishes and wear it down. Produce moisture or dryness and heat and
coolness according to what imbalance is to be corrected; it is in environments we
find the answer to your hands pressing together.

All is divine *and* human, I mean what does not have its own nature?
Silly to call sacred incidents not understood or known how to proceed in relation to.

We have no need of unprovable assumptions as we get too much introduced to those who talk of the sky and of what is below the earth; therefore say what you please but don't ask me to go along with what can't be disagreed with to any purpose.

Ma Rainey tours the Acropolis

Tomorrow is scattered mutilation
now I'm used to be by myself
it's bad enough, yeah, but
don't give me no drink in this murdering town.

Upon learning that she whom he would like to be his girl has been seeing some other man for a longer length of time than might be expected based on the evidence at hand Parmenides envisions the relation between elements and phenomena

If my tissues don't find me, at length
truncated

will be the coming-to-be of perishable things

where
everything is smaller and more so simultaneously

I find it
hard to accept the not-yetness of situations

or how to put aside the appearances of the ordinary

heaven
help my wrong devouring and the unencumbered

*   *   *

Empedocles to a cocktail waitress, "there is not death—there is only mingling of parts, so
why not?"

She returns, "what do you know, saying 'the everlasting can't undergo change,
or suffer pain and grief'?
What do you know to say 'there is no attendance in vacancy'?
It is only running out your bar tab that will bring your head upright."

Empedocles somewhat chagrined offers,
"if being were in more than one part it would have motion, and
if it had motion it could not Be; let's dispense with the illusion that our parts are not one."

She laughs and over her shoulder says,
"tonight's last call is all we have to count on,
at any rate
coition is a slight attack of epilepsy and I'm in no mood to shake about."

II

HOLLERS

I can study rain
oh, ohm drive, oh, oh, drive my blues
I been studyin' the rain and
I'm 'on drive my blues away
Goin' to the 'stil'ry
stay out there all day

— Robert Johnson,
"Preachin' Blues (Up Jumped The Devil)"

Pythagoras: one poem

Cosmology

would that the sea were the earth's sweat

and the magnetic stone had soul
for the iron it sets in motion

would that all were held together by numbers

would that it seemed imprudent
to urinate in the direction of the sun

would that there were first the counter-earth
would that then the earth and after that the moon

would that they bobbed in aether

would that the navel were an anchor
against the toss and wander

would that air lives in the death of fire
and water in the death of air

would that the first animals were made
in moisture and covered with prickly skin

Domestic Partner Blues (Take One)

My sexuality puts me in the top half of one
percent

but I have labored too theoretically and
I'll never fill in that head of
household bubble on my income tax,

as for now, sometimes

my domestic affection gets the
better of me—I know I could use more

legislature in my life, even if

you with a body grown lighter with all the
emptiness it has imprisoned has

not overcome our processes of
interlocking parts

despite the fact that

my consumer confidence is at an all time
fair-to-middlin.

Domestic Partner Blues (Take Two)

You say you have not been cheatin
but

your proof is the reality of sensory qualities,

our differences of surface rhythm
and inclination,

and arrangement,

they don't look overcomeable by
mere natural affection and class antagonism;

that is to say: your body is concave and mine sharply hooked,

and, you ain't be doing me right.

Empedocles: one poem

Cosmic Harmony and its Antagonist

It takes a little while to move a thought of the heart organ
to a practice of the limbs—

those members which are fitted together
which go too increasingly on their course for me.

Anaxagoras: two poems

Of Blood and Bone / A Final Premise

Original mixture and the seeds of things
ain't for me to know why

got me sleeping in the kitchen,
the undeterminable possibilities of change,

Just as welcome to fast from wickedness
and, gone ahead

make a mess of it and
personify the elements to alleviate my brain.

Qualitative Pluralist Love Song Blues

i.

Tax man's comin and cares not a bit
that it is the giant sky that binds
all constituents in its embrace,
not a bit that appearances are a
glimpse of the unseen, but anyway

Got me a scattered thought to reassure
Got me a divided mind to rest between

Got me everything but a way to put it.

ii.

Rent man's callin and says he won't take even
one of the red-hot bricks that puncture the night
to keep a cover over my head,
take none of the so-called mixing and
departing of real entities, yet, anyway

Got me a scattered thought to reassure
Got me a divided mind to rest between

Got me everything but a way to put it.

iii.

Bank man's knockin and heeds little the
moon as a mass of breath congealed as hail is,
little why what is called "birds's milk" is the
white of the egg, little how all the same, all
components partake of one another, and anyway

Got me a scattered thought to reassure
Got me a divided mind to rest between.

On Nature and Being

Woke up this morning gone right out of my head,
Drunk too much it looks to happen any
Kind of other way;
I'd still argue that there is no such stuff as emptiness
But my skull and pocket might disagree.

Spent my last dollar on something I can't remember
I believe I'll go back home,
I'll stay there and stay there unsatisfied, like
The apparent "how things are" that comes and goes.

Epistemology is a sweet skinned woman
And I know material can't be rubbed away
But my sole has a hole in it that don't see it at all that way.

I have no feet to get me to the station
I have no money to move on down the road
But soon as I find a new way to think through experience
You won't see me around here no more.

Zeno: one poem

reductio ad absurdum

for Parmenides

At the Lyceum they said
ten minutes ago a suicide bomber blew up a fuel truck near a police station

but it doesn't matter

they said

Those who were standing in the open were killed
Those who saw it were killed
at least nine people immediately
and sixty-two still have a good chance at it,

later you'll tell me that it was just the steel recognized at home

later you'll find me hunched and shirtless mulling over your distrust of what is called becoming
and you'll mention my arrows that do not fly,

it will make you want to demonstrate our lack of difference with those portions of us that
look the same so that creation and destruction are driven away
and later you'll say you're leaving me
and you'll tell me it doesn't matter

But if that's true, how is it that I feel so finite in number honey?

The Way of Inquiry

Who has a penicillin shot for me?
What is there that I am not willing to pay more than what it is worth for?
When can I be forgotten of all that is moveable as an unmovable term?
Where do I get my parking validated?
Why do dogs bark at people whom they do not know?
How is it that I wasn't born better looking and with
more smarter brains?

Selected Fragments

I've been neglectful [..................] of what I do
when awake as I've been just now [ ] well
I know say even numbskulls are workers and

[collaborators in] but I can't [
convince myself [..............] I'll see that
which is before me tomorrow [Whether I might]
[faithfully explain] [......] or do justice to
Where I put my common grips and grasps

had I a mind to—the [
point of philosophy is then [perhaps]
to get out of doing dishes
[..]

] I've [

[looked] on ambivalence unflinching [known]
numerous ontological paradox and

each was as luscious as the last [...] except
[Christ] [.....................] [well]
] I know there is

                                        ] a certain comfort in
                                        ] a cramped leg
                                        ] A certain pleasure in
tripping in public [
contentment at the idea of Homer flogged
in the street [on the whole] [.........]

      ] I've thought [

[the world holds] as much [
[ill] as good [   ] well [

nature plays us hide-and-go-seek and [
[I've thought intelligibility] a detail of economy
[..................] [And] [.....................]
that all my lovers have been a fine example

Relativity and Paradox Holler

Never gotten early up and out of bed, I'm never out of bed
apart from for the gals who need a ride one place or another
where I'm always being both glad and not glad to go;

always my wisdom
is found best in figuring, sort of, in thinking
I'm better off not having been happened upon
in more than a year,
each time even still thinking
what it is to stay awhile longer in that comfort,
and how best to get up and on out of here,
where I'm always being both glad and not glad to go;   each time
always
its usefulness
is always less for me having done something
like nothing
where I'm always being both glad and not glad to go.

Archelaus: one poem

Paternity Blues

History is a possible one-of-three—Daddy
and, even its nothing is too much to bear.

Hippocrates: two poems

The Sacred Malady

Having found such alleged origins as these
inadequate

those foundational propositions that fail to generate
the nature of particulars

Can't
seem to fit into what they are obliged to be like

What

lay nearest,

I think

What is not fire nor soil nor
any corporeal ingredient, can't be a proper cause,

nor should be reckoned one—

why

certain astonishments like chance, rather than
volition

should serve to explain problems of plausibility
more like what-comes-before

in not-coming-before terms.

On Ancient Medicine

after Skip James

Recognizably the silliness of too much education to hold a job;
Officially the harebrained trouble of being the genre convention of watching yourself
    watch yourself go shopping;
Properly the hope that there is a measure of constancy in events that have zero to do with us;
Technically if I could get a kind of first-principle perspective on the matter;
As a rule a hope to pass off indifference as a sense of humor;
Scientifically I've been judgmentally impaired and I've been sodden;
Concretely the joke that you might feel actually bad about some other place tearing itself apart;
Formulaically if my flesh brought suit against its soul the outcome is little to be guessed at;
Perchance the absurdity of the sun being made new each day;
Clinically notwithstanding socio-economic reality, we are all just trying to get by, and, that
    seems to finish it.

Xenophanes: one poem

The work song that we can't bring ourselves to write

A word like, "chthonic," meaning

adj: of the underworld; "nether regions,"

makes it too easy

to make a joke of Hell.

Alcmaeon: two poems

Genesis and Change

This body is not really like my body
had

I known you were going to be looking at it

I would have treated it much
better:

it has occurred for me most often
someplace

additional to the existing one,

I mean, its steerage

you know

its usefulness
is most suited to general ecologies

or circumstance,

but is not so much
equipment for several exacting activities.

State Security Jam

after Little Junior

Last night, I heard mama she told papa
I heard papa he told mama
I heard mama, she was talking to papa
about something she heard—
she told papa we've
had reporting to the effect that the sun made fight upon the earth, made
the heavens transparent, and the earth dry

papa he said

sweet little thing
sweet as you'll ever see—don't believe a word, we're goin boogie.

Mama she says
what is happening, what's happenin—
I hear, I heard
two long-standing equalities of power
are sifted off from one another,
when I understand better why in terms of
how and what we're,

papa he goes

sweet, sweet little thing
we're goin boogie.

What is happening, What's happenin, mama she said,
I don't feel good, I don't
last night, from what I heard
I heard, I hear, the former unravels, the latter skids and slinks
why we have to—I heard, I hear
why you don't know, can't confirm
occasionally there are, I hear, I heard—

papa he says

sweet little thing, don't believe a word
we're goin boogie tell the break of day.

When it Rains it Pours

(thinking of Billy "The Kid" Emerson)

Concerning my membranes,

whatever,

we perish is the matter:

It ain't right

to have make me pay

What is not directly traceable I'd like to stick my finger in its eye,

who's got troubles like the kind of me—not
counting those below the boundary decided for the national poverty line

—my seat of

distinguishing understanding

from perception

my little risk

yet, it's been my sense we deal largely in what is less than

science, or slaughter

The Unlimited and the Limiting

To test a hypothesis with somebody else's body
lying down with him
to see if you can tear God to pieces

Otherwise, try to make pussy the grounds for
assertions and conditions
when they are dismemberment
and unsupported by reason

as happens to most of us

Walking home

Heraclitus mutters,
"muddy river round my feet
muddy river round my feet
muddy river round my feet
take right hold of me."

Acknowledgements

I read widely on Greek philosophy while working on these poems, but I drew primarily on Philip Wheelwright's *The Presocratics,* and I am indebted to this text both for its commentaries and its language, including the Heraclitus quote used on the back cover. The image of Democritus's universe on the cover is taken from Mary Acworth Orr's *Dante and the Early Astronomers*, and the image of text is taken from Discovery's *Philosource* website. Thanks to the editors of *Mandorla, damn the caesars, BlazeVOX*, and *The Cultural Society* for first publishing versions of poems in this volume. Thanks as well to Joe Biel, Roberto Tejada, Kim Evans, Nathan Goldberg, Richard Deming, and Nancy Kuhl, who first and regularly responded to the poems as they were written.

Chax Press is located in the Tucson Historic Warehouse Arts District, in the Small Planet Bakery Building. Please contact us at *chax@theriver.com*, and visit our web site at *http://chax.org*, where you will also find the chaxblog. In August 2009 we celebrate our 25th birthday. Chax Press receives support from the Tucson Pima Arts Council, and from the Arizona Commission on the Arts, with funding from the State of Arizona and the National Endowment for the Arts. We depend on donations from readers like you, and you may give to Chax Press on our web site, or contact us for more information. Here are some of our recent titles; many more are found on our web site.

Jacque Vaught Brogan, *ta(l)king eyes*
Jeanne Heuving, *Transducer*
John Tritica, *Sound Remains*
Patrick Pritchett, *Salt, My Love: A Ballad* (handmade letterpress book arts work)
Kathleen Fraser and Nancy Tokar Miller, *Witness* (handmade letterpress book arts work)
CA Conrad, *The Book of Frank*
Michael Cross, *In Felt Treeling*
Steve McCaffery, *Slightly Left of Thinking*
Karen Mac Cormack, *Implexures* (complete edition)

TUCSON PIMA ARTS COUNCIL
Arizona Commission on the Arts
NATIONAL ENDOWMENT FOR THE ARTS